B-Roll, Transitions & Visual Effects Guide

Make Your Videos Look Professional With Creative Visual Styles

By Joe Correa

Published by Live Stronger Faster

This book is for educational and informational purposes only. The author and publisher are not engaged in rendering legal, financial, or other professional advice. Readers should consult a qualified professional before making any financial decisions.

First Edition

www.ingramcontent.com/pod-product-compliance
Lightning Source LLC
LaVergne TN
LVHW022012200926
848481LV00007B/2359
* 9 7 9 8 2 9 5 4 7 2 2 8 2 *

Table of Contents

Introduction

The world of modern content creation has shifted far beyond simply placing a camera in front of your face and hitting record. Today's viewers expect more than a message—they expect an experience. They want energy, emotion, movement, and visual stimulation that keeps them watching longer than they intended. They want videos that look "expensive," even when the creator filmed them on a phone and edited them with free apps. And at the center of that transformation lies one of the most important—and most misunderstood—elements of filmmaking for YouTube, Instagram, and TikTok: the mastery of B-roll, transitions, and visual effects. This book exists because the modern creator is now a hybrid artist, part filmmaker, storyteller, editor, visual designer, and content strategist all at once. And one of the fastest ways to elevate your videos into the top 10% is to develop a deep understanding of how to use supplemental footage, camera movement, dynamic transitions, and purposeful effects to make your message more compelling. Viewers may not consciously analyze your shots or transitions, but they instantly feel the difference between a video that flows beautifully and one that feels flat. In a world where attention is the most valuable currency, mastering visual enhancement is no longer optional—it is the key to getting noticed, remembered, and shared. Creators from every niche—real estate, fitness, beauty, education, lifestyle, tech reviews, travel vlogs, business tutorials—are discovering that the smallest changes in B-roll, pacing, and motion graphics can dramatically increase watch time, which then boosts algorithmic reach. A simple overhead shot of hands demonstrating something, a slow-motion clip of a workout movement, a macro shot of food ingredients, a cinematic drone reveal, or even a three-second close-up of your laptop keyboard can take a bland segment and elevate it into something atmospheric and emotionally resonant. B-roll acts as the visual language behind your narrative. It explains what words alone cannot. It fills the gaps between frames that would otherwise bore viewers. It gives texture, mood, rhythm, and personality to your videos—especially when used with intention rather than randomly. And when paired with transitions that feel smooth, natural, or creatively disruptive, your content immediately communicates professionalism, flow, and confidence.

This book is designed to demystify the entire process of creating stunning B-roll, choosing the right angles, building transitions that feel cinematic, and applying visual effects that enhance—not distract—from your message. Many creators make the mistake of copying random transitions they see trending online, using whip pans, zoom effects, or glitch overlays simply because they look "cool." But mastery comes from understanding *why* certain transitions work, how they match your pacing, how they influence viewer psychology, and when minimalism actually outperforms complexity. Some of the most viral content on social media uses extremely simple transitions—hard cuts, match cuts, jump cuts—executed with precision and rhythm. Others use advanced VFX sequences involving masking, motion tracking, or dynamic camera reveals. The goal of this book is to give you the full spectrum of knowledge so you can choose the right tool for the right moment and develop your own unique visual style.

In the age of AI, creators now have powerful tools like CapCut, InVideo, and Adobe Express that allow them to generate visual effects, animate text, create masking transitions, or enhance footage with a single click. But while these tools offer a shortcut, they cannot replace your eye for composition, your understanding of movement, or your intuition for what keeps a viewer emotionally engaged. AI will amplify your creativity—not replace it. This book will teach you how to use both manual and AI-assisted techniques to capture better footage, build sequences that flow naturally, and apply effects with purpose. You will explore how to storyboard your B-roll even when filming spontaneously, how to create movement without expensive gimbals, how to use shot variety to develop pacing, how to color grade your clips for mood, and how to use music and sound effects to elevate your visuals. Every chapter equips you with a system—not just inspiration—so you can apply these principles immediately to your next video.

A polished visual style also communicates authority. Viewers subconsciously associate professional transitions, clean B-roll sequences, and cohesive effects with higher-quality creators—creators they can trust, creators they are more willing to learn from, buy from, and follow long-term. Whether you are building a personal brand, producing tutorials, teaching a skill, reviewing products, or simply documenting your life, the level of craftsmanship behind your visuals matters. You don't need Hollywood equipment to make your content cinematic. You don't need to hire a team or buy expensive software. You simply need to understand the techniques that professionals use and adapt them to your niche, your personality, and your platform.

In this book, you will discover the psychology of visual movement, the science of viewer retention, and the creative techniques that make your content stand out. You will learn how to capture footage that enhances your story rather than repeating it. You will explore the power of transitions as emotional connectors—tools that signal meaning, shift tone, reset viewer attention, and guide the eye through your frame. You will learn how to choose the right visual style for your niche, how to avoid over-editing your videos, and how to build a consistent aesthetic across all your platforms. By the time you finish this book, you will be able to create sequences that look intentionally designed, not randomly assembled. You will know how to film B-roll that elevates your narrative, transitions that feel seamless, and effects that look polished instead of overwhelming. And most importantly, you will know how to bring your ideas to life with clarity, confidence, and a personal creative identity that viewers recognize instantly.

This is your guide to visual storytelling. This is your map to cinematic content. This is your opportunity to separate yourself from the average creator struggling to keep viewers engaged. By mastering B-roll, transitions, and visual effects, you gain the power to shape how your audience feels, what they focus on, how long they stay, and how deeply they connect with your message. Every video you create after this book will look more professional, more intentional, and more memorable. You are about to discover the tools and techniques that top creators use to transform simple footage into high-impact visual experiences—without complicated gear, without a film degree, and without spending thousands of dollars. You already have the camera, the ideas, and the ambition. This book gives you the cinematic language to bring it all together.

Chapter 1

The Power of B-Roll: How Supplemental Footage Transforms Your Entire Video

B-roll is one of the most misunderstood yet most powerful tools in modern content creation, and its proper use separates amateur videos from truly cinematic ones. At its core, B-roll is any supplemental footage that visually supports, enhances, or replaces your main "A-roll" talking footage. But the real power of B-roll comes not from the clips themselves, but from what they do to the audience's brain. B-roll prevents viewer fatigue, increases retention, reinforces complex ideas, and adds emotional tone to moments that would otherwise feel flat. Whether you're teaching, entertaining, demonstrating, or documenting, B-roll becomes the visual storyteller that fills the gaps no words can fill. To master B-roll, you must first understand that every clip has a purpose, whether it is contextualizing your environment, illustrating your process, providing emotional texture, or intensifying dramatic tension. When creators simply insert random stock clips or shoot meaningless footage just to "add something on the screen," they lose the opportunity to shape the viewer's feelings and expectations. Real mastery means capturing supplemental footage that feels intentional, relevant, and seamlessly integrated into the story you're telling—even if your story is a thirty-second Instagram Reel.

The first step to powerful B-roll is developing a habit of visual thinking. Instead of imagining the shots you want only while filming, you begin imagining them before you ever pick up your phone. Visual thinking involves asking the right questions: What is the viewer supposed to feel here? What do they need to see to understand this moment better? What movement or angle would enhance this idea? What details of your location, subject, action, or object would add interest to the scene? Filmmakers do this instinctively because they think in images, often building sequences in their heads before the camera even rolls. You do not need to be a traditional filmmaker to develop this skill—you simply need to practice observing your environment through a storyteller's eye. Depending on your niche, these visuals might be tight macro shots of hands working, wide establishing shots of your room or studio, medium shots of equipment, dynamic angles of objects in motion, or slow pans across textures, fabrics, landscapes, or technology. Every shot should add clarity, emotion, energy, or beauty.

Once you begin thinking visually, the next step is learning shot variety. Many creators rely only on wide shots or handheld medium shots, which quickly become repetitive. By incorporating a combination of wide, medium, tight, macro, and detail shots, you create rhythm and visual interest that subconsciously pulls the viewer deeper into your content. Shot variety also makes editing easier because it gives you options for transitions, pacing changes, and thematic emphasis. B-roll is also the easiest way to hide jump cuts or mask mistakes in A-roll, allowing your footage to feel more natural and professional. A simple cutaway to hands, an object, the environment, or a reaction can instantly smooth out a rough cut. Master creators understand that B-roll gives them editorial flexibility while also elevating the emotional tone of a scene. For example, a motivational video might use slow-motion footage, soft lighting, and gentle camera movement. A tech tutorial might rely on crisp macro shots, whip-pans, and dynamic angle changes. A travel vlog might use sweeping wide shots combined with transitional camera passes. Each style communicates a different emotional language.

Another crucial aspect of B-roll mastery is movement. Whether the camera moves or the subject moves, motion naturally captures attention and helps guide the viewer's eye. Movement makes even simple scenes feel alive. That movement might come from a pan, tilt, slide, push-in, pull-out, orbit, handheld sway, or even small purposeful micro-movements that mimic the feeling of human observation. You don't need expensive stabilizers or sliders to create this effect—your smartphone, your body, and intentional breathing are often enough to produce cinematic-looking footage. AI editing tools like CapCut can stabilize shaky shots, add motion blur, or even animate static images, but the foundation comes from how you shoot. Every movement should have intention. A slow push-in might indicate importance or seriousness, while a fast whip pan might communicate energy, humor, or urgency. Understanding how movement impacts viewer psychology gives your B-roll a deeper purpose and helps you stand out among creators who shoot their supplemental footage with no strategy at all.

Lighting plays an equally important role. No matter how creative your angle or how smooth your movement, bad lighting will sabotage your B-roll. When filming supplemental footage, always look for soft, directional light—window light, shade outdoors, diffused lamps, or indirect sunlight. Good lighting adds depth, clarity, and mood to your footage, allowing your viewers to see the details that make your video feel richer and more polished. Harsh overhead lighting can make objects look flat and unappealing. Backlighting can create silhouettes that work artistically but often reduce clarity. Using simple tools like white foam boards, reflective surfaces, or even a smartphone's screen as a reflector can dramatically improve your results without requiring professional gear. Visual storytelling thrives when lighting is intentional and supportive rather than accidental. The editing stage is where your B-roll truly comes alive. This is where transitions, pacing, sound design, and color adjustments elevate raw footage into cinematic sequences. Before you drop in random clips, ask yourself what each shot accomplishes. Does it visually explain a concept? Does it provide a moment of calm between explanations? Does it shift emotional tone? Does it set up the next scene? B-roll should never distract from your main message; it should highlight it. Editing also becomes easier when you structure your B-roll into sequences rather than isolated clips. A sequence is a mini-story—multiple shots of the same action, location, or object capturing different angles, movements, and details. Sequences give your videos natural continuity and make transitions smoother because the viewer expects visual progression. For example, a coffee sequence might include a wide shot of the table, a medium shot of the hand grabbing the mug, a close-up of steam rising, and a tight shot of the pour. These shots can be combined to create a visually satisfying moment that builds atmosphere and connects emotionally with your viewer.

Finally, mastering B-roll is about building habits. Keep your phone ready. Capture details wherever you go. Build a personal library of clips that match your style. Pay attention to the world around you—the textures, colors, movements, objects, and environments that tell visual stories. The more intentional you become, the more cinematic your content feels, and the more viewers will engage with your videos. B-roll mastery is not about equipment or software—it is about awareness, creativity, and the commitment to enhancing your message with purposeful visual language. Once you understand that B-roll is a tool of persuasion, emotional connection, and narrative elevation, you unlock one of the greatest advantages a creator can have in today's fast-moving digital world.

The Footage That Changed Everything

When Mia first picked up her phone to film videos for her small fitness brand, she believed all she needed was good information and a confident voice. She had watched hundreds of creators go viral seemingly overnight, and she was convinced the difference between them and her was luck. So she recorded her A-roll—straight-on shots of her explaining exercises, nutrition, and motivation—and waited for the viewers to arrive. But they didn't. Her videos stalled at a few hundred views, and even those who clicked barely made it past the halfway mark. Mia didn't realize it at the time, but what she lacked was the very thing her audience needed most: a visual experience that pulled them into her world. The moment that changed everything came one Saturday morning when she watched a creator break down a simple workout tutorial using dynamic shots of hands adjusting dumbbells, sneakers hitting the ground, sweat dripping down arms, close-ups of tightening laces, and crisp transitions between angles. The A-roll wasn't much different from hers—but the B-roll carried the emotion, energy, and impact. Mia realized something powerful: people don't just watch content—they feel it.

Determined to improve, she grabbed her phone and started filming the little details of her routine. She filmed the way sunlight hit her water bottle. She captured slow-motion clips of her resistance bands snapping into place. She recorded tight shots of her shoes, her stopwatch, her workout mat unfolding. She took wide overhead shots of her gym corner and close-ups of her hands demonstrating movements. For the first time, she wasn't filming because she needed content—she was filming because she was starting to see her world differently. Every texture, movement, and angle felt like a visual puzzle piece waiting to belong to something greater. She didn't know the terminology yet. She didn't understand shot composition or lighting theory. But she had discovered the most important skill any creator could develop: the ability to think visually and record intentionally.

Her first video using B-roll felt different even before she uploaded it. Editing suddenly became more exciting. She layered her A-roll explanations with cutaways that illustrated her points. She added a soft zoom and a slow pan across her equipment to build atmosphere. She played with pacing, giving viewers a moment to breathe between her explanations. She wasn't just creating a tutorial now—she was crafting an experience. When she hit "publish," she expected her usual slow start. But within hours, comments began to appear. People mentioned how satisfying the visuals were. How clear her explanations felt with supporting footage. How cinematic the shots looked even though she filmed everything on her phone. Mia didn't realize it yet, but she had just crossed the invisible threshold between creator and filmmaker.

Encouraged, she began filming B-roll every day. She captured sunrise jogs, street reflections on rainy days, dumbbells resting against hardwood floors, and steam rising from her morning tea. Mia started to understand how B-roll didn't just complement the story—it could *become* the story. The more she filmed, the more she developed an instinct for what her audience wanted to feel. She learned that movement created energy, that detail shots gave intimacy, and that wide shots built context. She discovered that slow-motion could heighten emotion, while fast-paced sequences could add urgency. Her visuals began to match the spirit of her message, and viewers responded with loyalty she had never experienced before.

As her community grew, Mia received invitations to collaborate with brands, fitness apps, and gyms. Everyone praised her "professional-looking videos," asking which camera she used or who edited her clips. She would smile because the truth still surprised her: it was all her phone, her hands, and her newfound understanding of B-roll. The visual language she once ignored had become the very foundation of her creative identity. She no longer relied solely on talking-head footage. Instead, she let visuals tell half the story.

Months later, while preparing a video on confidence and self-worth, Mia felt something profound. She realized her journey wasn't about mastering equipment or learning software. It was about learning to see her world with intention—to find meaning, beauty, and narrative in the smallest moments. Every shot she captured carried a piece of her growth. Every transition reflected a new level of clarity. Every sequence represented the creator she had become. Her content wasn't just better—it was more human, more expressive, more alive. And her viewers felt it.

In the end, it wasn't a viral trend or a lucky algorithm push that changed Mia's career. It was the moment she understood that B-roll was not filler—it was storytelling. It was emotion. It was identity. It was the bridge between information and impact. For Mia, mastering B-roll didn't just improve her videos—it transformed her entire approach to creativity. She finally understood what successful creators knew all along: your audience may not remember your exact words, but they will always remember how your visuals made them feel

Chapter 2

Camera Movement: How Motion Creates Emotion, Flow, and Visual Energy

Camera movement is one of the most effective ways to elevate your B-roll and create videos that feel cinematic, intentional, and emotionally compelling. When used correctly, movement can guide the viewer's eye, shape the tone of a scene, enhance storytelling, and control the pacing of your content. When movement is absent or accidental, videos tend to look static, lifeless, or amateurish. But when movement becomes a deliberate part of your visual strategy, even simple shots filmed with a smartphone can feel like scenes from a professional production. The most important principle to understand about camera movement is that movement must have meaning. Every pan, tilt, orbit, slide, push, pull, or handheld sway communicates something psychological to your audience. Whether you realize it or not, the way your camera moves is influencing how viewers interpret your message and how long they continue watching.

One of the core functions of camera movement is to create visual interest and maintain audience engagement. Humans are wired to pay attention to motion. It signals life, relevance, and energy. In a digital environment where the viewer can swipe away in less than one second, movement becomes a tool of retention. A slow push-in can create a sense of importance or introspection, subtly telling viewers that what they're looking at matters. A pull-out can widen context or signify transition. A lateral slide can mimic exploration or curiosity. Even a gentle handheld sway can add warmth and personality to your content because it feels natural and human. These movements don't require expensive gimbals or professional rigs. In many cases, your hands, arms, and body can create smooth, cinematic motions when you move with intention and maintain steady breathing. With practice, your body becomes the stabilizer, allowing you to film dynamic, fluid shots that captivate your audience without drawing attention to the movement itself.

Understanding how movement shapes emotion is equally important. Different movements evoke different feelings, and skilled creators choose motions based not only on aesthetics but on the emotional tone they want to convey. A slow pan across a quiet room communicates calmness, reflection, or intimacy. A quick whip pan between two subjects creates energy, humor, or urgency. A low-angle forward push can convey power, dominance, or excitement. An orbit around a subject adds drama and dimensionality, making the viewer feel like they are physically exploring the scene. Movement must match message. A fitness creator demonstrating a high-intensity workout might use fast-paced movements, quick cuts, and high-energy swoops. A meditation teacher might favor slow, drifting motions with minimal distractions. The key is not just knowing how to execute movement—it is understanding how to strategically align movement with mood, message, and viewer expectations.

Movement also plays a critical role in how you structure your transitions. Transitions look their best when they match the motion of the preceding shot. If your camera whips to the right at the end of one clip, cutting to another shot that begins with a rightward whip will create a seamless flow. If your camera pushes in at the end of a scene, transitioning into a clip that begins with forward motion feels natural and professional. Motion-matched transitions are one of the most powerful tools in video editing because they trick the viewer's brain into feeling continuity, even when switching between completely different locations or subjects. This technique is used constantly in films, travel videos, product reels, and high-performance social content. Understanding how to integrate movement at the shooting stage will make your editing drastically easier and your final video far more polished.

To master camera movement, you must also master stability. Viewers can tolerate movement, but they cannot tolerate accidental shake that feels chaotic or amateurish. Smooth motion is created through control. You can lock your elbows, tuck your arms close to your body, walk heel-to-toe, glide your steps, brace your phone against your chest, use a neck strap for stabilization, or rotate your torso rather than your wrists to maintain clean motion arcs. Movements should be deliberate and consistent from start to finish. A shaky motion can work stylistically for certain niches—like intense sports edits or chaotic humor—but it should be a creative decision rather than a mistake. Tools like gimbals, tripods, sliders, and stabilizing grips can help, but you do not need them to create professional results. The creator is always more important than the gear.

Another powerful aspect of camera movement is guiding viewer attention. When you move the camera toward an object, you signal importance. When you move away, you indicate transition. When you move alongside a subject, you create identification—viewers feel like they are experiencing the world beside the subject. Movement can also hide imperfections or give depth to scenes that would otherwise feel flat. Even a simple vertical tilt from a tabletop surface up to a laptop screen can reveal context in a visually satisfying way. A horizontal slide across a cluttered desk can become a sequence if you capture the same motion from multiple distances.

Movement creates possibilities. It offers rhythm. It builds anticipation. And when you combine motion with shot variety, lighting, and intentional composition, you create B-roll that truly looks professional.

Finally, creators must learn to slow down movement. Too many beginners rush their motions, making footage jittery, rushed, or inconsistent. Smooth movement requires patience, control, and breath. Even fast transitions should begin with shot captures that are clean and predictable. Move slowly, breathe steadily, and let motion flow naturally. The camera is not meant to replace expression—it is meant to enhance it. When used correctly, camera movement becomes your voice, your rhythm, your silent narrator guiding viewers through your world. Mastering it will transform your content from simple clips into immersive, emotionally resonant visual experiences. This single skill—understanding how your camera moves—can instantly elevate your storytelling, editing, and on-screen presence, placing your work leagues above creators who simply point and record without intention.

The Walk That Changed the Shot

Lucas had always considered himself a storyteller. From the moment he started creating product review videos for his small tech channel, he believed the power of his content lived in his words—his explanations, his clarity, his passion for gadgets. And for a while, it worked. His small audience appreciated his honesty and the thoroughness of his reviews. But deep down, he knew something was missing. His videos lacked the visual quality that other tech creators effortlessly delivered. Their footage felt alive. Their transitions were seamless. Their products seemed to float in space with cinematic flair, while Lucas's shots looked rigid, static, and uninspired. He tried new lighting and improved his audio, but something still felt flat. He didn't understand the problem until the day he took a simple walk that changed everything.

He was reviewing a pair of noise-canceling headphones and decided to film outdoors for a change. As he walked through the park, he absentmindedly filmed the headphones swinging in his hand. The camera moved with his steps—smooth arcs, gentle forward momentum, shifting sunlight dancing across the matte finish of the ear cups. When he returned home and watched the footage, something clicked. That accidental motion gave the clip life. It felt cinematic, immersive, almost like a commercial he might see from a major brand. Without planning it, he had captured movement that felt intentional. For the first time, his footage looked better than he expected. Lucas replayed it several times, realizing a truth that would transform his entire creative process: it wasn't the product that made the shot interesting—it was the motion.

From that moment, Lucas became obsessed with camera movement. He began practicing simple motions in his living room—slow push-ins toward his desk, gentle pull-outs from his computer setup, lateral slides across the edges of keyboards and mousepads, tip-toe half-orbits around standing objects. He discovered how slightly bending his knees added smoothness. How rotating his torso instead of his wrist created steadier arcs. How holding his breath during key movements removed micro-shake. Every new discovery made his shots more fluid, more intentional, more beautiful. He filmed the same objects dozens of times, learning how different movements created entirely different emotions. A slow upward tilt made his desk setup feel majestic. A fast whip toward the speaker controls added excitement. A drifting handheld sway turned an ordinary monitor shot into something atmospheric.

The first video he created using these techniques shocked him. Suddenly his B-roll felt like it belonged in a commercial. His transitions matched the motion of his shots perfectly, creating a level of polish he had never achieved before. Viewers noticed immediately. Comments poured in saying his production value had skyrocketed. People assumed he bought a new camera or hired an editor. Lucas smiled as he read every comment, because the truth was far simpler—he had just learned how to move with intention.

As his channel grew, Lucas began exploring outdoor walks intentionally. He filmed earbuds bouncing in sunlight, power banks sliding into backpacks, and tablets tucked under his arm as he walked past city murals. Movement became the heart of his creative identity. He stopped filming products like static objects and began filming them as characters within environments. Movement created emotion, and emotion created connection. He no longer needed expensive gear to compete with the top creators in his niche—his mastery of motion did the heavy lifting.

Months later, Lucas reflected on his journey as he prepared to film a review of a new smart watch. He stepped outside, took a slow breath, and let his camera follow the natural movement of his body. Every shot felt alive. Every motion felt purposeful. He had learned that camera movement wasn't just about technique—it was about awareness. It was about recognizing the beauty in motion and using it to guide the viewer's experience. His content no longer felt flat or stagnant. It resonated. It breathed. It lived.

For Lucas, the walk through the park that day wasn't just exercise—it was revelation. It taught him that movement is emotion, and emotion is what keeps viewers watching. The moment he embraced motion, everything about his videos changed. He had unlocked a new level of storytelling, not through new equipment or complicated effects, but through the simple act of learning how to move with intention. And the viewers could feel it.

Chapter 3

Transitions: How to Move Between Shots With Flow, Style, and Purpose

Transitions are far more than decorative effects placed between two clips. They are one of the most essential storytelling tools in video production because they determine how your video "feels" as it moves from moment to moment. A transition is the invisible glue that binds your scenes together, controlling pace, flow, emotional shifts, and audience retention. Beginners often treat transitions as add-ons—something to sprinkle on top of footage for flair or personality. Professionals treat transitions as part of the language of filmmaking, using them intentionally to communicate meaning. Whether you're creating YouTube tutorials, TikTok edits, Instagram Reels, travel videos, fitness content, or product demos, your transitions help your audience stay connected to the narrative. A strong transition is almost never noticed consciously. Viewers simply feel that the video flows beautifully. A weak transition stands out immediately, breaking immersion and reminding the viewer they're watching something edited. Once that happens, attention drops, and your video risks losing its momentum.

The foundation of effective transitions begins in the filming stage with movement, shot alignment, and composition. The biggest mistake creators make is trying to "fix" transitions during editing when the real issue is the footage itself. A transition works best when the motion, direction, lighting, or shape from the first shot matches or complements the second shot. This is known as motion matching. For example, if one shot ends with your camera moving upward, cutting to a second clip that begins with an upward motion creates seamless flow. If the first clip ends with a rightward pan, starting the next shot with a rightward pan preserves continuity. These natural transitions feel effortless because your viewer's brain registers the motion as one continuous action. This technique dramatically increases the perceived quality of your videos. It works for simple clips, complex sequences, slow-motion shots, and fast-paced edits. The key is intentional shooting. When you capture B-roll with transitions in mind, every movement becomes a stepping stone to something greater.

Beyond motion, transitions can be created through shape, color, light, or object alignment. For instance, cutting from a circular object to another circular object creates a visual match. Transitioning from a bright light source in one scene to a similar highlight in another creates cinematic unity. Moving from a close-up shot to another close-up creates emotional continuity. Even simple hard cuts become transitions when executed with alignment and rhythm. This type of editing—cutting on action, cutting on shape, cutting on motion, cutting on sound—is what gives professional videos their polished feel. In the world of short-form content, where pacing is everything, these micro-transitions matter more than flashy effects. Algorithms reward retention, and retention grows when transitions keep viewers visually stimulated without overwhelming them. This is the delicate balance you will learn to master.

Once your footage is structured properly, you can use stylistic transitions to enhance your edit. These include whip pans, zoom transitions, match cuts, speed ramps, masks, spin transitions, glitch effects, wipe transitions, object reveals, and many more. AI-powered editors like CapCut can apply these transitions instantly with presets, but the principle remains the same: the transition must serve the story. A whip pan adds speed, energy, and urgency. A zoom transition creates excitement or drama. A speed ramp intensifies momentum. A masked transition feels clever and creative, often used in travel and fashion videos. These techniques work beautifully when used sparingly and intentionally, but they can also ruin a video when overused. Flashy transitions draw attention to themselves. They shout. They demand focus. Which means your story must match that intensity. Using a dramatic spin transition in a calm, reflective video breaks emotional tone. Using a soft fade during a high-energy montage can flatten your pacing. Every transition has an emotional purpose, and knowing when *not* to use something is just as important as knowing how to execute it.

Sound plays an equally important role in transitions. Audio can hide cuts, intensify movement, or create anticipation. Cutting on a beat makes your transitions feel intentional because the viewer subconsciously expects something to change at moments of rhythmic emphasis. Swooshes, swipes, digital clicks, or ambient sound resets can create auditory bridges between clips. Sound elevates your visual transition because the brain combines the senses to interpret meaning. This is why top creators align their transitions to music—even minimal ones. When the cut matches the sound, it feels cleaner, tighter, and more professional. Without sound, even well-shot transitions may feel flat or incomplete. Great editors treat audio transitions with the same respect they give visual transitions because together, they create the immersive experience that keeps viewers watching.

The ultimate purpose of transitions is to guide your viewer through your video without friction. If a transition calls too much attention to itself, distracts from the subject, or breaks emotional continuity, it fails. Transitions should clarify, enhance, and support your message—not overshadow it. This is why many high-performing creators use fewer fancy transitions as they mature. They learn that a perfectly timed hard cut can be more powerful than any effect. They learn that rhythm, pacing, and visual alignment matter more than technical tricks. They learn that transitions are not about impressing the viewer—they are about elevating the story so the viewer forgets the editor exists. This is the invisible art of seamless editing. The goal is always the same: flow, emotion, clarity, and engagement. Master these principles, and your transitions will elevate your entire visual identity.

The Cut That No One Noticed

Jasmine had always admired the creators whose videos felt effortless. She didn't understand how they made everything flow as if the camera floated from moment to moment without ever breaking rhythm. Her own videos felt choppy and disconnected. Each clip felt like a separate idea rather than part of a unified story. She spent hours adding flashy transitions—spin effects, glitch reveals, digital wipes, zoom bursts—hoping one of them would make her content feel smoother. But the more transitions she added, the messier everything looked. One night, after posting another video that barely reached a few hundred views, Jasmine sat at her desk feeling defeated. She had the passion, the creativity, and the desire to improve—but something in her editing process wasn't clicking.

Everything changed when she stumbled upon a behind-the-scenes edit from one of her favorite travel creators. In the video, the creator explained that the secret to great transitions wasn't the effects—it was the footage. He showed how he intentionally filmed the end of one clip with a rightward camera movement and the beginning of the next clip with the same direction. Jasmine watched in awe as he layered the two shots back-to-back, creating a seamless flow that felt invisible. He didn't add a single transition effect. No fancy whip. No digital spin. Just a perfect match in motion. Jasmine sat back in her chair, stunned. She realized she had been fighting the wrong battle all along. She was trying to force transitions in editing instead of setting them up while filming. That revelation felt like a spark in her mind. It was the moment she understood what her videos were missing.

The next morning, Jasmine walked through her neighborhood with her phone in hand, determined to rethink her approach. She practiced simple movements—slow pans, gentle tilts, forward pushes, sideways slides—memorizing how each felt in her hands. She filmed the end of one shot swinging slightly to the left, then filmed the next beginning with the same motion. She captured objects that matched shapes, colors, or movement patterns. She filmed the golden reflection of the sun on a window, then cut to the warm glow of a candle. She recorded her feet stepping forward, then cut to her hand opening a café door with the same forward momentum. For the first time, she saw transitions not as effects, but as moments of continuity. When she returned home and began editing, something magical happened. Her footage finally "talked" to itself. Clips connected. Scenes breathed. Every transition felt natural, effortless, invisible. She removed almost all her old flashy transitions and replaced them with motion-matched cuts. She aligned her edits to the beat of her background music, creating rhythm where there had previously been chaos. She added subtle swooshes and ambient resets to smooth out difficult cuts. She used visual alignment and emotional pacing to create moments that felt like one continuous journey. And when she posted the video, she watched her analytics in disbelief. Viewers stayed longer—much longer. Comments filled her feed with, "Your editing has leveled up," "This flows so well," and "I don't know what you changed, but this feels amazing."

That night, Jasmine replayed her video again and again, realizing that the best transitions were the ones no one noticed. The ones viewers couldn't explain but felt deeply. She finally understood that transitions weren't decorations—they were storytelling devices. They were the beats between the notes, the breath between ideas, the gentle bridge from one moment to the next. They were the invisible hand guiding the viewer's attention without demanding recognition. And now that she could wield transitions with purpose, her entire creative identity began to evolve. Weeks later, Jasmine filmed a travel vlog in a new city. She no longer chased flashy transitions. Instead, she chased continuity—matching colors, movement, direction, and emotion throughout her shots. Her footage flowed like water, and editing became a joy rather than a struggle. She trusted her instincts. She trusted the story. Most importantly, she trusted the subtle power of transitions to shape her viewer's experience. Her videos began attracting more views, more engagement, and more opportunities. But the greatest reward was something far deeper: she finally felt like her videos expressed the creator she always knew she could be.

Jasmine's breakthrough didn't come from a new effect or a new piece of gear. It came from understanding that great transitions are invisible because they serve the story, not themselves. And as long as she honored the story, her transitions would always guide her audience smoothly from one moment to the next—one seamless cut at a time.

Chapter 4

Composition & Framing: How to Build Cinematic Shots With Intention and Visual Design

Composition is one of the most transformative yet overlooked elements in video creation. While lighting and camera movement shape how your footage feels, composition determines how your footage is understood. It is the art of placing subjects, objects, and visual elements in a frame in a way that communicates clarity, emotion, depth, and professionalism. In photography and filmmaking, composition is the silent architecture that organizes a viewer's attention. Most viewers don't consciously notice great composition, but they instantly sense when something feels balanced, pleasing, or cinematic. Conversely, bad composition feels amateurish even when shot in 4K with perfect lighting. This is why understanding composition is one of the most essential skills you can develop as a creator. You may have the best transitions, the smoothest camera moves, and the strongest B-roll ideas—but if your composition isn't intentional, your shots will never reach their full potential.

Composition begins with the ability to direct the viewer's focus. The number one question every creator should ask before recording any shot is: *What do I want the viewer to look at first?* In every frame, there should be a clear subject—the hand picking something up, the device being demonstrated, the environment you're introducing, the texture you're highlighting, the motion you're capturing. Without a visual anchor, the viewer's eye wanders aimlessly, which creates confusion and reduces engagement. This is why creators rely on foundational composition techniques such as the rule of thirds, leading lines, center framing, and directional balance to guide attention. These tools aren't meant to restrict your creativity—they're meant to give you control over how your viewer experiences your shot.

The rule of thirds divides the frame into nine equal rectangles using two vertical and two horizontal lines. Placing your subject along these lines or at their intersections creates natural visual tension and balance. This technique prevents static, centered shots from feeling boring or lifeless. However, center framing has its place as well—especially when communicating power, simplicity, directness, or symmetry. Leading lines draw the viewer's eye toward your subject, which is especially useful in product shots, desk setups, architecture, or any environment with natural patterns. Framing your subject with surrounding objects—doorways, windows, mirrors, hands, or props—adds depth and layers. Foreground elements create a sense of immersion by giving the viewer the feeling of being inside the scene rather than observing from a distance. These techniques allow you to craft shots that feel intentional, cinematic, and emotionally connected to your story.

Depth is another crucial element of cinematic composition. Flat shots lack dimension and visual interest. Depth gives your footage life. You can create depth through layers—foreground, subject, and background—and by using angles that create diagonal lines rather than flat, straight-on perspectives. Even slight angle adjustments can transform a boring shot into a dynamic one. Depth can also be created by lighting, shadows, color contrast, and selective focus. Smartphones today have excellent depth-of-field modes, but real depth comes from how you arrange your scene. A plant in the foreground, a laptop in the midground, and a window in the background can instantly create a rich, visually appealing frame. Combined with a slow push-in or drift, depth becomes one of the strongest tools in your cinematic toolkit.

Another powerful compositional tool is negative space—the intentional empty space around your subject. Negative space adds breathing room, conveys minimalism, and creates emotional tone. It can be calming, mysterious, or strong depending on how you use it. TikTok, Instagram Reels, and YouTube Shorts benefit greatly from negative space because it reduces visual clutter and keeps the viewer focused. Long-form content, like YouTube videos, can also use negative space to emphasize important moments. Creators often overlook negative space because they feel compelled to fill the frame with objects, but cinema thrives on restraint just as much as fullness. The balance between space and subject gives your visuals rhythm and personality.

Composition also works hand-in-hand with color and geometry. Color contrast can guide the viewer's eye more powerfully than movement or lighting. Warm colors pull attention forward while cooler colors recede. High contrast adds intensity, while low contrast creates softness. Even prop placement influences composition. A bright red object in the background can distract from your subject unless you intentionally use it as a visual anchor. Likewise, symmetry can communicate order, structure, and beauty when executed with intention. Many viral videos gain popularity not because of their subject matter but because the compositions feel satisfying to the human brain. Clean lines, color harmony, geometric patterns, and controlled framing all signal professionalism—even in simple shots.

The final piece of composition is consistency. When your shot composition shifts erratically from one clip to another, your video feels disjointed. When your framing choices are intentional and consistent, your video feels cohesive. Consistency doesn't mean every shot must look the same. Rather, it means every shot should feel like it belongs to the same visual language. This is what creates a recognizable "style." Some creators use tight, intimate frames. Others prefer wide, airy compositions. Some emphasize symmetry; others embrace controlled chaos. Whatever style you adopt, the key is intentionality. Every frame must reflect a choice rather than an accident.

Composition is far more than placing objects in a frame—it is visual storytelling. It determines how your viewer feels, where they look, how long they stay engaged, and how they emotionally interpret your message. Mastering composition will elevate every part of your video production process, from B-roll to transitions to long-form scenes. It is the foundation of cinematic content. Once you learn to compose your shots intentionally, your videos will begin to look dramatically more professional—even if you film everything using nothing more than your smartphone.

The Frame Within the Frame

Daniel had always been fascinated by filmmaking, but when he began creating content for his small clothing brand, his videos never looked the way he imagined. He had the right lighting. He had smooth camera movement. He edited with clean transitions and trendy effects. Yet something about his footage always felt off—flat, lifeless, and strangely empty. He didn't understand why until one afternoon when he walked into a local art gallery. He stood in front of a painting that captured a simple scene: a window, a desk, a cup of tea, and sunlight stretching across a wooden floor. It was nothing extraordinary, yet the composition drew him in. The window framed the light, the desk framed the cup, and the shadows framed the entire scene. It was a frame within a frame. A quiet moment made powerful through intentional placement. And in that moment, Daniel realized what his videos were missing: composition.

The revelation hit him harder than he expected. He immediately went home, grabbed his phone, and began studying every frame he had filmed over the past few months. He saw the mistakes clearly now—subjects placed randomly, empty spaces cluttered with distractions, angles that flattened his clothing pieces instead of giving them shape. His videos lacked visual purpose. Determined to change, he cleared a space in his small studio and began experimenting with compositions in the most basic way—placing a single shirt on a table and trying to frame it differently. He tested wide shots, tight shots, overhead shots, angled shots, framed shots through doorways, and even shots with foreground elements like plants or books. For the first time, he saw how drastically composition changed emotion.

He then began applying these lessons to his next clothing campaign. Instead of filming his shirts on a hanger, he laid them on textured fabric, positioning them along the rule of thirds. He angled his camera slightly to introduce depth. He used a plant leaf in the foreground to add layers. He framed one shirt between two open wardrobe doors to create a sense of discovery. He let sunlight pour across a folded hoodie, creating shadows that added dimension. Every frame became a painting. Every clip told a visual story. Each shot he captured felt more intentional, more expressive, more alive than anything he had filmed before.

When Daniel edited the footage, he felt something shift. For the first time, his video looked like a commercial. His shirts stood out with clarity and emotion. The backgrounds no longer distracted; they supported. His framing decisions created rhythm and cohesion. The footage flowed not because of fancy transitions or effects but because each frame felt connected through visual harmony. When he posted the final video, the response stunned him. Viewers commented on how "clean," "professional," and "satisfying" his visuals were. Sales increased. Collaborations appeared. His brand suddenly looked bigger than it was.

But the moment that changed him most came later, while filming a behind-the-scenes clip for his audience. He placed his camera on his desk and instinctively positioned the frame so the doorway created a natural border on one side and a soft plant shadow filled the other. As he hit record, he realized something profound: composition had become instinctive. He no longer thought about rules; he thought about meaning. He no longer positioned objects randomly; he placed them with intention. His studio looked different because he now saw it through a filmmaker's eyes.

In the months that followed, Daniel's content evolved dramatically. He found beauty in angles he never used before. He embraced negative space and symmetry. He used color contrast to highlight textures. He framed moments through shelves, mirrors, chair backs, and windows. His videos no longer felt like simple product showcases—they felt like experiences. Composition had become his visual signature.

What Daniel learned in that art gallery transformed his entire creative journey. It taught him that professionalism isn't about expensive equipment or complicated effects. It's about seeing. It's about intention. It's about arranging the world inside the frame in a way that guides emotion and tells a story. In the end, Daniel realized that composition wasn't just a technical skill—it was a way of communicating without words. And once he mastered that language, everything about his videos—and his brand—changed forever.

Chapter 5

Lighting for B-Roll & Effects: How Light Shapes Mood, Depth, and Cinematic Quality

Lighting is the backbone of cinematic video production, and when it comes to B-roll and visual effects, it becomes even more essential. Light determines the clarity, depth, color, mood, and emotional tone of every shot. Without intentional lighting, even the most beautifully composed footage will fall flat. With proper lighting, even simple objects become stunning, three-dimensional, and visually rich. Most creators underestimate lighting because they rely solely on their environment. But the difference between amateur and professional visuals rarely lies in the camera—it lies in how the scene is lit. Light is not just illumination. It is storytelling. Every shadow, highlight, reflection, and gradient communicates something to the viewer. To master B-roll and cinematic visuals, you must learn to control light—or at least learn to recognize environments where the lighting works for you rather than against you.

The first principle of lighting for B-roll is direction. Light coming from the front creates even illumination but flattens the subject. Light from the side creates shadows, shape, and dimension. Light from behind creates silhouettes, glows, halos, and dramatic contrast. Soft, diffused light creates a gentle, pleasing look with minimal harsh shadows. Hard light creates contrast, intensity, and strong edges. The direction of your light will determine whether your footage feels calm, dramatic, energetic, mysterious, or intimate. Side lighting is often the most cinematic, revealing texture and form. Backlighting is excellent for mood, atmosphere, and transitions. Front lighting can be used strategically for product reveals, beauty shots, or high-key tutorials. Every clip you film should begin with one question: *Where is the light coming from, and what is it doing to my subject?*

The second principle is softness. Soft light is the secret weapon of cinematic visuals. When light is diffused through clouds, curtains, softboxes, or white reflectors, it spreads evenly across your subject, reducing harsh shadows and creating gentle gradients. Natural window light is one of the best sources of soft light available to creators because it offers both beauty and directional control. Shooting B-roll near windows, open doors, shaded outdoor areas, or diffused lamps will instantly upgrade your footage. Harsh overhead lights—common in kitchens, garages, and offices—can ruin your visuals by casting unflattering shadows and flattening your subject. You can soften overhead lighting by turning it off and replacing it with side-facing lamps, bounce cards, or LED panels pointed toward walls. Even a white piece of foam board can act as a powerful reflector to create cinematic softness.

The third principle is contrast. Contrast gives your footage depth, separation, and emotion. Low-contrast lighting feels calm, modern, and bright. High-contrast lighting feels intense, dramatic, and textured. This is why cinematic scenes often feature a strong key light on one side and a darker shadow on the other—known as "short lighting." This technique sculpts your subject visually, creating three-dimensionality on screen. When shooting B-roll of products, faces, hands, or textures, controlling contrast becomes essential. Too little contrast makes everything look washed out. Too much contrast makes details disappear. The goal is to find the ratio that matches your visual style. Creators who focus on energetic content (tech, fashion, sports, travel) often use higher contrast to create pop. Creators who focus on lifestyle, wellness, cooking, or education often use softer, more even lighting.

The fourth principle is color temperature. Every light source has a temperature measured in Kelvin—from warm golden hues to cool blue tones. Mixing color temperatures unintentionally can ruin your footage. Shooting near a window (cool daylight) combined with warm indoor lamps creates muddy, unattractive color shifts. Clean, cinematic shots use consistent color temperature. Decide whether you want a warm tone or a cool tone and adjust your environment accordingly. Turn off lights that don't match. Add small LED panels, lamps, or bounce cards to reinforce one temperature. Many creators choose warm lighting for cozy, emotional content and cooler lighting for sleek, modern content. You can also use color-intentional lighting—RGB lights, neon accents, or colored gels—to add personality, atmosphere, and thematic style to your B-roll.

The fifth principle is light separation. Separation means ensuring your subject stands apart from the background. A backlight or rim light behind your subject adds a glow that visually separates them from the environment. This is especially important when filming dark objects against dark backgrounds or brightly lit subjects against bright backgrounds. Without separation, your subject blends into the frame. With separation, your subject becomes the clear focal point. This single technique is responsible for much of the "studio-quality" look viewers associate with professional filmmakers. Even a small lamp pointed toward the wall behind your subject can create separation.

The final principle is lighting consistency. When your lighting changes drastically between clips, your video loses cohesion. Smooth editing and cinematic visuals rely heavily on consistent lighting across your B-roll sequences. That doesn't mean every shot must look identical, but they should feel like they belong together. Using the same window, the same lamp, or the same color temperature maintains unity. Editing tools like CapCut, Final Cut, or DaVinci Resolve can fix minor inconsistencies, but foundational lighting decisions must be made during filming. The more consistent your lighting, the easier your editing becomes—and the more your final video feels polished, intentional, and visually professional.

Lighting is not just a technical element—it is an emotional tool. It shapes the viewer's experience before your story, script, or transitions ever begin. By mastering the principles of direction, softness, contrast, color temperature, separation, and consistency, you gain cinematic control over every piece of B-roll you capture. Even if you film everything with a phone and a single light source, knowing *how* to use that light will elevate your content instantly. Lighting is where creators stop looking like beginners and start looking like filmmakers.

The Light Behind the Curtain

Sofia had always been proud of her cooking videos. She poured her heart into every recipe, every chop, every simmer of the pot. But no matter how delicious her food was, her videos simply didn't look like the polished cooking content she admired online. Everything she filmed looked dull. Her vegetables looked lifeless. Her countertops looked gray. The steam rising from her dishes barely showed. She had tried new angles, better cameras, trendy editing effects—nothing worked. Her visuals refused to pop. One afternoon, while scrolling through her favorite creator's behind-the-scenes stories, she noticed something she had always ignored: the light. The creator filmed everything next to a giant window, with soft sunlight pouring across the cutting board. It made every ingredient glow. It added life to the footage. Sofia paused the video and whispered to herself, "It's the light."

That single moment sent her into her kitchen to experiment. She dragged her wooden cutting board toward the window. She opened the curtain to reveal soft late-afternoon light. She placed a bowl of cherry tomatoes on the board and looked through her phone's camera. Her breath caught. The tomatoes glistened. Shadows curved softly across their surfaces. The wooden grain looked warm and textured. It was the most beautiful footage she had ever filmed—and she hadn't even turned on the stove. For the first time, Sofia understood what her videos had been missing. It wasn't the camera. It wasn't the angles. It wasn't the editing. It was lighting. And she could control it.

From that day forward, lighting became her obsession. She woke up early to observe how morning light spilled across her kitchen counter. She watched how cloud cover softened the harsh midday sun. She experimented with lamps, white towels as reflectors, and even the flashlight on her phone bounced off a wall to create soft side light. She discovered that her kitchen's overhead lights ruined her visuals, so she turned them off and relied instead on side lighting from the window. She began to understand that light had texture, direction, temperature, and shape. It wasn't just brightness—it was emotion.

Her first fully lit video felt like magic. The steam rising from her soup became a glowing ribbon of light. The knife slicing through onions created tiny prisms that sparkled. The olive oil coating her pan turned into liquid gold. Even simple steps—washing herbs, mixing batter, stirring broth—looked cinematic. Viewers noticed immediately. Comments flooded in: "Your videos look beautiful!" "How is your lighting so perfect?" "This feels like a cooking show!" Sofia laughed at the irony. Nothing about her setup felt professional. It was still just her kitchen, her window, and a few makeshift reflectors. But she now saw her kitchen the way a filmmaker would—not as a place to cook, but as a place to craft stories with light.

As weeks passed, lighting became instinctual. Sofia would walk into a room and immediately see where shadows formed and where highlights fell. She rearranged her kitchen to optimize the light flow. She placed white boards near her stove to bounce light onto pots. She used warm lamps to create cozy evening scenes and cool morning light for crisp breakfast recipes. Every adjustment enhanced the mood. Her lighting choices became part of her storytelling. Bright, airy light for refreshing summer salads. Warm, golden light for nostalgic comfort food. High-contrast shadows for dramatic chocolate desserts. Light had become her secret ingredient—one that no recipe included but every viewer could taste.

Months later, when a cooking brand reached out to collaborate, they complimented her on the "professional studio lighting" she must have been using. Sofia smiled to herself. Her "studio" was still the same small apartment kitchen with the same single window, the same curtains, and the same wooden cutting board she had owned for years. The difference wasn't equipment—it was vision. She had learned to see the world the way filmmakers do: through the language of light.

The moment Sofia mastered lighting was the moment she finally fell in love with her own videos. She realized that lighting wasn't a technical burden—it was a creative playground. It let her shape emotion, highlight beauty, and bring her cooking to life in ways she never thought possible. The curtain she once overlooked had become the key to unlocking her cinematic identity. And every time she pulled it open, she felt like she was letting in more than sunlight—she was letting in possibility.

Chapter 6

Color & Mood: How Color Grading and Palette Selection Shape Emotion, Style, and Visual Identity

Color is one of the most powerful emotional tools in filmmaking, and when used with intention, it becomes the defining element of your video's mood, style, and identity. Viewers often cannot explain why certain videos feel warm, nostalgic, energetic, modern, or dramatic, but they can instantly sense it. Color works on a psychological level, triggering emotional associations faster than words, music, or movement. A warm orange tone can evoke comfort, friendliness, or inspiration. A cool blue tone can communicate calmness, modernity, or seriousness. High contrast can create intensity and excitement, while low contrast invites softness and serenity. In short: color is storytelling. And for creators who want to develop a recognizable visual brand, mastering color grading is essential.

Before you touch any color-grading tools, you must first think about color in the filming stage. The colors inside your frame—the objects, walls, clothing, props, backgrounds, and lighting—are the raw ingredients that your grading will enhance. If your environment is chaotic, with clashing colors or mixed lighting temperatures, your footage will be harder to grade cleanly. This is why many professional creators intentionally simplify their environments or use palettes that complement each other. A food creator might lean into warm wood tones, golden highlights, and earthy colors to create appetite and warmth. A tech creator might lean into cool grays, blues, and blacks to create a sleek, modern look. A fitness creator might emphasize high contrast and vibrant colors to communicate energy. The point is to shoot with your intended color mood already in mind.

Once your footage is captured, color grading becomes the process of refining tone, adjusting balance, enhancing mood, and aligning the visual feel of your clips. The most important step in color grading is achieving consistency. Different clips filmed in different locations or lighting conditions will naturally have different color casts. Color grading brings them into harmony. This harmony creates a sense of professionalism and narrative unity. Whether you use CapCut, DaVinci Resolve, Final Cut, Premiere, or mobile apps, the core principles remain the same: neutralize unwanted color, adjust exposure, set your contrast curve, define your color temperature, and then enhance the mood. Even subtle adjustments can transform footage from ordinary to cinematic. The first task is basic correction—fixing what the camera captured incorrectly. This includes adjusting white balance to ensure whites look white, blacks look black, and skin tones look natural. If white balance is incorrect, the entire color palette will shift in an undesirable way. The second step is exposure control—ensuring highlights aren't blown out and shadows aren't crushed. Balanced exposure gives you more room to shape the final look. Once these foundational corrections are in place, you can begin shaping mood with curves, hue adjustments, and selective color grading. Curves control contrast, and contrast controls emotion. Increasing contrast adds punch and intensity. Decreasing contrast makes your footage feel soft and dreamy. Manipulating shadows and highlights allows you to push warmth, coolness, or stylistic color tones into your footage.

After contrast, the next layer is creative color grading. This is where you shape your visual identity. You might add teal shadows and warm highlights for a cinematic blockbuster feel. You might use soft pastel tones for aesthetic lifestyle content. You might create deep blacks and poppy colors for action footage. You might create desaturated backgrounds with vibrant subjects for product B-roll. The key to creative grading is subtlety. Beginners often push colors too far, creating unnatural or overprocessed footage. Professionals aim for balance, harmony, and emotional nuance. A great color grade enhances your story without screaming for attention. Finally, you must consider your brand identity. Over time, your viewers should begin to recognize your color style. Maybe your content always has warm shadows. Maybe your greens are slightly desaturated. Maybe your blues are cooler than average. Maybe your highlights have a soft gold tint. These small stylistic choices become your trademark. They help viewers remember you. They create continuity across your videos. They separate your brand from the millions of creators who use default color profiles. A strong color identity builds trust and memorability. And once you've defined your palette, color grading becomes easier, faster, and more intuitive.

In the end, color is more than an aesthetic choice—it is emotional language. It determines how your audience feels before they even register what they're watching. By learning to control color, you learn to control mood, atmosphere, storytelling, and brand identity. And once you master color grading, your videos will feel richer, deeper, and more cinematic—regardless of the camera or software you use.

The Color She Didn't See

Aisha had been creating travel videos for almost a year, and while her editing was improving, something about her footage always felt off. Her shots were clear. Her camera movement was smooth. Her transitions were crisp. But when she compared her videos to the cinematic travel creators she admired, hers felt strangely lifeless. Their oceans were turquoise and glowing. Their sunsets were golden and soft. Their city nights sparkled with neon vibrancy. Meanwhile, her footage—captured in the same types of locations—looked flat, grayish, and dull. She didn't understand why until one evening, she watched a behind-the-scenes breakdown from her favorite travel filmmaker. He said something that struck her deeply: "You're not filming places—you're filming color."

The idea consumed her. She opened her past videos and paused them frame by frame. She noticed how many clips had mixed color temperatures—cool daylight from windows, warm tungsten streetlights, strange green casts from restaurant bulbs. She noticed how her clothing clashed with the environment. She noticed how shadows were often too dark or highlights too blown out for any color to feel rich. Most painfully, she realized she had never truly looked at color as something she could control. She simply captured what was there. She saw the world but never saw its colors.

Determined to change, she began studying color with a childlike curiosity. She walked outside at sunrise to study the warm golden tones. She observed how shadows turned blue in the late afternoon. She noticed that ocean water looked completely different depending on whether the sun was behind or in front of her. She realized that cloudy days created soft, neutral palettes perfect for skin tones, while harsh noon sun created extreme contrast. She discovered that restaurants with neon signs could be cinematic if she leaned into their colors instead of fighting them. She started choosing her outfits based on color harmony with her location. She even bought a small white card to help her set accurate white balance.

Her next trip was the turning point. She traveled to Lisbon with a plan—not just to film the city, but to film its colors. She wore muted earth tones so the pastel buildings would stand out behind her. She filmed in the early morning to capture the warm glow of the rising sun. She shot at blue hour to capture the rich deep hues of the sky. She avoided mixed lighting by turning off indoor lamps and relying on window light. She filmed shadows intentionally, not accidentally. Every frame she captured felt like a painting.

When she returned home and began color grading, her footage responded beautifully. Her curves created depth. Her warmth added emotion. Her shadows received a soft teal tint. Her highlights glowed with a golden hue she never knew how to create before. Every shot felt like it belonged to the same film. Every scene flowed visually. She couldn't believe these colors had been inside her footage all along—they had simply been waiting for her to learn the language of color.

When she posted the final video, she watched the comments roll in. “Your footage looks dreamy.” “What camera do you use now?” “This looks like a movie.” “Your color is unreal.” Aisha smiled because she knew the truth: her camera hadn’t changed. Her editing software hadn’t changed. Only one thing had changed—her ability to *see* color.

A month later, while filming a quiet alleyway at sunset, she paused her camera and looked around. The golden light bounced off the stone walls. The shadows layered into soft blue gradients. The terracotta rooftops glowed with warmth. It was beautiful, but not because the place was special. It was beautiful because she had finally learned to see its colors. And she realized the same was true for her videos. They were always capable of being cinematic. She just needed to understand the emotional language hidden inside every hue.

Color had become her guide. Her storyteller. Her silent collaborator. And every time she graded a video, she felt like she was painting her journey—not with brushes, but with light.

Chapter 7

Speed, Motion & Timing: How Slow Motion, Speed Ramps, and Rhythm Transform Cinematic Storytelling

Speed is one of the most underutilized tools in video creation, yet it has the power to reshape an entire narrative. Most creators think of speed simply as "slow motion" or "fast motion," but real mastery involves understanding timing, rhythm, pacing, acceleration, deceleration, tension, and release. When used skillfully, speed becomes a storytelling device that can elevate emotion, reveal hidden details, highlight key moments, and create dramatic visual impact. When ignored, footage can feel jarring, rushed, or unremarkable—no matter how good the composition or lighting may be. Speed is not just a technical setting; it is the pulse of your video.

Slow motion is one of the most powerful ways to transform ordinary footage into something cinematic. When you slow down movement, you allow viewers to appreciate the beauty, detail, and texture of a moment. Water droplets become suspended diamonds. Hair flips become graceful arcs. A jump becomes a ballet. Muscles, fabrics, shadows, and materials reveal details that the naked eye cannot fully perceive in real time. But slow motion is most impactful when used intentionally. Not every clip benefits from it. Slow motion works best when the subject contains natural motion—pouring coffee, running, slicing ingredients, turning pages, lifting weights, adjusting equipment, or performing actions with emotional or visual significance. The key is to slow down moments that matter, not moments that fill space. When overused, slow motion loses its magic.

Speed ramping—the gradual speeding up or slowing down of a clip—is one of the most professional-looking techniques a creator can use. A well-timed ramp creates a sense of flow, energy, and narrative momentum. Speed ramps mimic the natural rhythm of adrenaline, curiosity, and discovery. They allow viewers to feel the transition, not just see it. When ramping into a moment, speed builds tension. When ramping out of a moment, speed creates release. The best speed ramps follow the physical logic of motion—fast during transitions, slow during impact. This technique requires planning during filming. Smooth movement, consistent lighting, and deliberate camera motion create footage that responds beautifully to speed changes. Jerky or inconsistent shots become more distracting when speed is manipulated, so shot quality matters.

Timing is equally important. Every clip has a natural "emotional duration"—the amount of time a viewer needs to absorb it before it feels too long or too short. A beautiful slow-motion pour may need two to three seconds. A speed ramp zoom may need half a second. A transition may need a fraction of a second. One of the biggest editing mistakes beginners make is holding shots too long. The viewer loses momentum, and attention drops. Rhythm and pacing give your video life. Rhythm can be based on music, motion, action, or emotional beats. In short-form content, rhythm tends to be tighter and more energetic. In long-form content, rhythm allows more breathing room. Regardless of format, understanding how long to stay on a clip is one of the most important editing instincts a creator can develop.

Motion also interacts with speed. Shots filmed with smooth movement respond beautifully to slow motion and speed ramps. Shots filmed handheld often create jitter when manipulated. This is why capturing solid foundational footage is essential. When filming B-roll that you plan to ramp, shoot at high frame rates—60fps, 120fps, or 240fps—whenever possible. These higher frame rates allow you to slow down footage without losing clarity. Shooting at low frame rates and trying to slow down later creates stuttered, unnatural footage that feels amateurish. Speed effects must enhance the footage, not fight against it.

Speed also influences emotion. Slow motion evokes nostalgia, gravity, romance, and elegance. It creates a sense of timelessness and emotional weight. Fast motion creates energy, action, chaos, humor, or momentum. Speed ramps create anticipation and excitement. Cutting rapidly between fast and slow sequences creates contrast and helps build narrative arcs. Every speed choice signals something to the viewer. If your pacing is too slow, viewers become bored. If it's too fast, they become overwhelmed. The perfect pacing feels invisible—it carries the viewer effortlessly through the story without drawing attention to itself.

Finally, mastery of speed requires restraint. The greatest editors know when not to use slow motion, when not to ramp, when not to accelerate. Intentionality separates stylish videos from messy ones. When every moment has the same energy level, nothing stands out. When you strategically place speed changes only where the story benefits, each one becomes impactful. Speed gives your footage texture. It gives your story shape. It gives your video a heartbeat. And when used with precision, it becomes one of the most powerful tools in your creative arsenal.

The Moment That Slowed Down

Eli had always filmed skateboarding videos for fun, capturing his friends grinding rails, flying off ramps, and carving down city streets. He loved the chaos, the movement, the adrenaline. But when he edited his footage, it never had the same impact as the videos on his favorite skate channels. Those videos felt epic, cinematic, emotional—even spiritual. Theirs made you feel the ride. His made you watch it. He didn't understand the difference until one evening when he recorded a friend landing a clean kickflip as the sun dipped low behind the buildings. The light was perfect, the move was clean, and the city looked alive. When he slowed the clip down for fun, something magical happened. For the first time, the moment felt legendary.

The slow motion transformed the movement into something poetic. The board rose with grace, spinning in the air like it was weightless. His friend's shoes hovered with impossible precision. Dust particles floated in the glow of the sunset. Every tiny detail that real time hid became visible. Eli watched the clip again and again, mesmerized. He had captured hundreds of tricks before, but he had never felt one. Slow motion revealed the soul of the moment. And in that moment, Eli understood what had been missing from his videos all along: timing.

He began experimenting immediately. He filmed his friends launching off stair sets, grinding handrails, tapping curbs, and cruising down streets. But this time, he shot at higher frame rates. He positioned himself where the light painted shadows. He moved with the skaters instead of standing stiffly. He tested ready-made speed ramps in editing, discovering how they created energy and rhythm. He noticed how speeding up the approach and slowing down the impact made the trick feel more powerful. He noticed how ramping out of the moment gave viewers a sense of release. He noticed how the interplay of fast and slow created an emotional arc—anticipation, climax, exhale.

Every clip he edited taught him something new. Some tricks looked better in real time. Others needed slow motion. Some moments begged for speed ramps. Others needed stillness. He learned not to force speed changes where they didn't belong. He learned to listen to the footage. He learned that pacing was a kind of music—beats, pauses, crescendos, drops. His videos began to feel alive. For the first time, his edits matched the energy he felt when skating with his friends.

Then came the night that changed everything. Eli followed his friend Mateo to an abandoned parking garage where skaters gathered after dark. The air was cool, the concrete smooth, and the fluorescent lights buzzed overhead. Someone placed a portable speaker against a pillar, filling the garage with a low, thumping beat. Mateo tried a heel flip over a parking barrier, failing twice. On the third attempt, he landed it perfectly, sliding across the smooth floor with sparks of energy. Eli filmed the entire sequence without thinking—just instinct and rhythm guiding his hands. When he reviewed the footage at home, he knew he had captured something special. He applied a speed ramp to the exact moment Mateo's feet connected with the board. The motion slowed beautifully. The beat aligned perfectly. The lights flickered in the background. Eli felt chills. It didn't look like a skate video—it looked like a story. A moment of triumph. A moment no one else had witnessed with the same intensity.

That video changed his channel. People commented on how cinematic it felt. How emotional. How "real." They weren't just watching tricks—they were experiencing them. Brands reached out. Other skaters asked to collaborate. But more importantly, Eli felt like he had finally captured what he had loved all along—the emotional truth of skateboarding.

He realized that speed wasn't just about visual flair. It was about feeling. It was about slowing down the moments that deserved reverence and speeding up the transitions that carried the story forward. It was about using timing to make ordinary moments extraordinary. It was about shaping rhythm to reflect the heartbeat of the scene.

And every time Eli slowed down a clip, he remembered the first moment he truly *felt* a kickflip—the moment the city paused, the board floated, and time stretched itself long enough for him to see beauty hidden inside the motion.

Chapter 8

Visual Effects & Enhancements: How Subtle Effects, Overlays, and Motion Graphics Elevate Your Story Without Overpowering It

Visual effects, when used with intention, can transform your videos into polished, dynamic, and emotionally compelling works of art. While many beginners associate “VFX” with flashy transitions, explosions, or dramatic animations, professionals understand that visual effects are most powerful when they enhance rather than distract. The purpose of VFX is not to draw attention to themselves but to elevate the story, improve clarity, emphasize mood, and guide viewer attention. In modern content creation—especially short-form videos—effects like overlays, light leaks, glows, digital noise, particle effects, chromatic aberration, masked transitions, animated text, and motion graphics have become essential tools for shaping cinematic identity. However, real mastery comes not from knowing how to add effects but knowing when, where, and why to use them.

The foundation of strong VFX work is subtlety. Even the most dramatic effects should feel integrated, not pasted on top of the footage. When effects overpower the content, they break immersion and signal inexperience. When used artfully, they create cohesion, atmosphere, and emotional resonance. Start by thinking of effects as seasoning—small creative touches that enhance flavor. A warm light leak adds nostalgia and softness. A subtle glow enhances elegance. A grain overlay adds texture and timelessness. A masked reveal adds clever storytelling. A touch of chromatic aberration adds a stylized edge. Each effect serves a specific emotional purpose. The key is choosing the right effect for the right moment, rather than using effects just because they look cool.

The next principle of VFX mastery is environmental matching. Effects must match the tone, lighting, color, and movement of the underlying footage. For example, adding warm lens flares to cold, blue-toned footage creates visual dissonance unless done intentionally. Overlays should complement existing light sources, not contradict them. Motion graphics should match the pacing of the edit. Color effects should support mood rather than fight against it. The more seamlessly an effect blends into the footage, the more cinematic the final product becomes. Many creators fail at VFX not because their effects are poorly chosen, but because they fail to integrate them properly. Integration is everything.

Another essential element of visual effects is realism—or at least the perception of realism. Even stylized effects must follow visual logic. Light leaks should appear from the direction of natural light. Particles should drift according to motion and environment. Glows should emanate from appropriate highlights. Masked transitions should align with object edges or natural movement. When effects follow physical logic, the viewer accepts them intuitively. When they violate that logic, viewers subconsciously sense something is "off," affecting how professional the video feels. The human eye is incredibly skilled at detecting inconsistencies in light and movement. Your job as a creator is to avoid triggering that discomfort.

Timing is equally critical in VFX. Effects must follow the rhythm of the edit. Placing a burst, flare, or motion graphic slightly too early or too late can break the flow. Effects should land on beats, impacts, transitions, emotional peaks, or moments of emphasis. They should feel like part of the narrative, not decoration. Well-timed effects can elevate transitions, intensify emotional moments, and create surprising visual delight. Poorly timed effects feel chaotic or distracting. As with speed and pacing, the best VFX timing feels invisible—effortless to the viewer because it harmonizes with the underlying rhythm of the story.

One of the most underrated forms of VFX is text animation. Animated titles, captions, lower thirds, and callouts can elevate your content dramatically when executed with intention. Clean typography, subtle motion, and cohesive style can make your content feel high-budget and well-produced. However, text should never compete with the visuals. It should reinforce meaning, guide the viewer, or enhance your branding. Motion should be smooth and purposeful. Many creators over-animate text in an attempt to appear modern, but excessive movement can distract from the story. The most cinematic text animations are often the simplest ones—gentle fades, minimal slides, soft scale-ups, or elegant reveals.

Filters, LUTs, and pre-built effects should be treated as tools, not crutches. They provide starting points, but true cinematic style comes from customization, careful adjustments, and intentional choices. Many LUTs are too strong out of the box. Overuse of built-in effects creates visual sameness. Your goal is to develop a unique visual signature by understanding how and why effects work. Create a consistent palette, a consistent glow style, a consistent noise level, a consistent overlay intensity. Over time, your audience will recognize your videos by their subtle cinematic fingerprint.

Finally, VFX mastery requires restraint and respect for storytelling. Effects must never replace strong footage, strong composition, strong lighting, or strong pacing. Their job is to enhance—not to patch weaknesses. When your visuals are already strong, effects elevate them into something memorable. When your visuals are weak, effects highlight the flaws. True creators use VFX thoughtfully, sparingly, and strategically. They understand that the most cinematic moment in a video is not made by effects but enhanced by them. When used with intention, visual effects can transform an ordinary scene into something unforgettable. But the moment you use effects to compensate for lack of planning, your footage loses authenticity. VFX should highlight emotion, amplify beauty, and elevate storytelling—not distract from it.

Mastering visual effects is not about learning hundreds of techniques. It is about learning how to blend them seamlessly into your narrative. When you understand the emotional purpose behind each effect, your videos gain depth, cohesion, and cinematic power. And when viewers feel that power—without even realizing why—they stay longer, engage deeper, and remember your content long after it ends.

The Glow in the Alleyway

Marisol had always been drawn to beautiful videos—the kind that shimmered with atmosphere, where light flickered through dust particles, where glows danced across the screen, where text floated effortlessly and transitions felt like magic.

But when she tried to replicate those effects in her own content, everything looked artificial. Overlays sat on top of her footage instead of blending into it. Flares looked fake. Animated text felt childish. Her videos looked noisy rather than cinematic. She assumed she simply wasn't talented enough to use effects the way the big creators did. But everything changed one night when she took a shortcut home down an alleyway she usually avoided.

The alley was damp from a light rain. Neon signs from a nearby restaurant bounced pink and blue reflections off puddles. A breeze carried a thin fog through the air. Marisol stopped walking. It was beautiful—unexpectedly beautiful. She pulled out her phone and hit record. Without thinking, she walked slowly, letting the neon reflections paint her frame. She filmed the fog drifting across the light. She filmed a glowing puddle rippling from a falling raindrop. She didn't apply effects. She didn't think of overlays. She just captured the moment exactly as it existed.

When she got home, she added the footage into her editing timeline and froze. The glow was already there. The atmosphere was already there. The depth, the shimmer, the mood, the emotion—it had all existed naturally. All her attempts to create these effects artificially suddenly felt misguided. The moment she saw her raw footage, she realized something profound: VFX aren't meant to create magic—they're meant to enhance it. Real magic starts in the moment you capture the scene.

Inspired, Marisol approached her next video differently. Instead of stacking random effects onto weak footage, she focused on capturing natural atmosphere—lamps through fog, sunlight through curtains, reflections on glass, dust floating in afternoon light. When she finally added effects, she used them subtly. A soft bloom on highlights to enhance warmth. A delicate grain overlay to add texture. A faint chromatic shift to emphasize motion. A gentle lens flare aligned perfectly with an actual light source. She was no longer forcing effects into the scene—they blended into it.

Her footage responded beautifully. For the first time, her effects felt like a part of the world she filmed. Her video glowed—not because she added glow, but because she enhanced the glow that was already present. Viewers noticed immediately. Comments flooded in. "These visuals are stunning." "Your style is so cinematic." "How did you get that neon glow?" Marisol smiled at the last comment. She didn't add the glow. She saw it—and enhanced it.

The breakthrough deepened her curiosity. She began studying how professional filmmakers matched effects to environment.

She noticed how light leaks always aligned with light sources. How grain matched the resolution of the footage. How color grading amplified mood rather than rewriting it. She began to see VFX as a dialogue between reality and creativity—never one overshadowing the other. A few weeks later, Marisol returned to the same alleyway. This time she brought intention with her. She filmed puddles, reflections, mist, and neon signs from multiple angles. She captured motion that could support masked transitions. She filmed her hand passing the camera to create natural wipes. When she edited the footage, everything aligned effortlessly. She added a soft glow that followed the neon lights. A particle overlay that matched the drifting fog. A color grade that enhanced the pink and blue tones. The final result looked like a music video—moody, atmospheric, immersive.

It became her most successful video yet.

But what mattered most wasn't the views—it was the realization that changed her identity as a creator. She no longer saw effects as shortcuts. She saw them as collaboration. The world provided beauty; she enhanced it. The footage whispered; the effects emphasized its voice. She finally understood why the best creators used effects sparingly: the story and the moment were already powerful. Effects existed to elevate, not overshadow.

From that night in the alleyway forward, every video she made began with the same question: "What magic is already here?" And once she answered it, she used effects not to replace reality—but to illuminate it.

Chapter 9

Sound Design: How Audio, Atmosphere & SFX Elevate Visual Storytelling

Sound design is one of the most underestimated components of cinematic content creation. While viewers often forgive imperfect visuals, they rarely forgive bad audio. Sound is the emotional anchor of your video. It shapes rhythm, creates atmosphere, emphasizes motion, enhances transitions, and brings B-roll footage to life. Without sound design, even the most beautifully shot visuals feel empty and disconnected. Great sound design, however, merges seamlessly with visuals to create immersion—a feeling that the viewer is not merely watching a scene but experiencing it. Sound is not just noise; it is storytelling. It contains the nuance, texture, and emotional charge that visuals alone cannot communicate.

The first principle of sound design is clarity. Your primary audio source—whether it's your voice, background dialogue, narration, or ambient sound—must be clean. Distorted, hollow, or muffled audio breaks immersion instantly. When viewers struggle to hear or understand what's being said, they disconnect. Clear audio begins at the source: speaking close to a microphone, eliminating echo, reducing background noise, and capturing sound with intention. In B-roll, clarity means capturing or enhancing atmospheric details that match the environment. The clink of coffee cups, the gentle brush of fabric, the crunch of footsteps, the whoosh of motion—all these small details make your visuals feel real. Even when you add sound effects in editing, the foundation of clarity ensures everything blends cohesively.

The second principle is atmosphere—what sound designers call "ambience." Ambience is the subtle background layer that fills space without drawing attention to itself. It gives context, depth, and emotional tone to a scene. A quiet room might include soft air hums, distant birds, faint wind, or the low resonance of the space. A city scene may contain distant chatter, traffic hum, footsteps, and environmental movement. Ambience is crucial because completely silent backgrounds feel unnatural and uncomfortable. Humans expect environmental sound, even if they do not consciously notice it. Adding a gentle, consistent atmospheric bed elevates your visuals into an immersive experience. Ambience also helps glue scenes together; even if clips are filmed in slightly different environments, a consistent atmospheric layer creates cohesion.

The third principle is motion. Motion sounds—swooshes, slides, swipes, whooshes, impacts, snaps, and transitions—enhance movement on-screen and amplify the visual rhythm. Motion sounds must be chosen carefully. They should match the speed, intensity, and emotion of the movement they accompany. A slow camera push might require a soft atmospheric swell. A fast transition might use a sharp whip. A product reveal might pair with a clean, crisp swipe. Overuse of motion sounds can overwhelm the viewer, so subtlety is key. The purpose is to support the movement, not overshadow it. When done well, motion sound creates an intuitive connection between audio and video, making transitions feel more polished and satisfying.

The fourth principle is emotional tone. Music is the emotional backbone of your video. The right soundtrack transforms ordinary footage into something meaningful. A soft piano piece turns a simple morning routine into a reflective moment. A cinematic swell transforms product B-roll into a powerful reveal. An upbeat pop track adds joy and energy. A moody electronic tone creates introspection. Music must align with the story and pacing—not fight against them. Volume must remain balanced so the music enhances rather than dominates. And depending on your narrative, silence or minimal sound can be just as powerful as music. Emotionally intelligent sound design means knowing when the viewer needs stimulation and when they need space to feel.

The fifth principle is synchronization. Sound must follow visual timing. Every cut, movement, transition, and action point must align precisely with audio cues. Syncing music beats to transitions creates flow. Syncing footsteps to actions creates realism. Syncing SFX to slow-motion ramps creates power. Poor synchronization creates discomfort; great synchronization creates satisfaction. When viewers say your editing "just feels right," what they're often responding to is audio alignment.

The final principle is layering. Great sound design involves multiple layers working in unison—ambience, effects, music, foley, tonal accents, and subtle enhancements. Each layer should be quiet enough to remain unnoticed individually but strong enough to contribute to the whole. Layering creates dynamic richness. It takes flat visuals and gives them dimensionality. Layering is what transforms a silent cooking clip into a rhythmic dance of chopping sounds, sizzling pans, soft clinks, and atmospheric warmth. It's what turns a fitness reel into a motivating burst of breath, movement, impact, and energy. It's what turns travel B-roll into a cinematic experience filled with wind, footsteps, leaves rustling, and environmental resonance.

At its core, sound design is emotional design. It is mood sculpted through frequencies. It is rhythm carved through timing. It is texture painted through audio layers. Mastering sound design means learning to listen—to the world, to your footage, and to the emotions you want your viewer to feel. When sound blends seamlessly with visuals, your content stops being a video and becomes an experience. And experiences are what viewers remember.

The Sound of the Streetlights

Noah never thought much about sound. He cared about visuals—the way light shimmered on wet pavement, the way neon signs cast colorful reflections, the way city buildings created towering silhouettes. But sound? He barely noticed it. When he edited videos, he usually muted clips and added music over everything. For him, visuals were the language of filmmaking. Until one night, sound changed everything.

It was late, and Noah walked home through the city after helping a friend film a music video. The streets were slick from a recent rain. Streetlights hummed. Cars passed softly in the distance. A train rumbled somewhere far away. Noah pulled out his phone almost unconsciously and began recording. But this time, instead of focusing on the imagery, he listened. He heard the layered ambience of the city—the endless symphony he had ignored all his life. The hums, the echoes, the drips, the footsteps, the hollow resonance of empty storefronts. The city didn't just look alive. It sounded alive.

When he got home and dropped the raw footage into his editing timeline, something surprised him. The visuals were nice—but the sound was breathtaking. It pulled him into the moment. It made the empty streets feel full. It made the stillness feel emotional. The sound of distant traffic warmed the scene. The faint buzz of a streetlight added tension. A single dripping gutter created rhythm. Without intending to, Noah had captured something he had never created before: *atmosphere*. And he realized this was what his videos had been missing.

Driven by curiosity, Noah began listening to his world the way a sound designer would. He recorded the crunch of leaves under shoes. The hiss of opening soda cans. The rustle of fabric during movement. The soft thud of books closing. The clink of his keys. The hum of refrigerators. The deep whoosh of stairwell doors. He layered these sounds over his visuals and suddenly everything felt alive. His footage transformed. People commented that his videos felt “immersive,” “cinematic,” “different,” though few could explain why. It was the sound.

But the moment that changed him happened a few weeks later. Noah filmed a short story about a lonely commuter waiting for a late-night train. He shot it at an old station under flickering lights. The visuals were moody and perfect, but it wasn’t until he added sound that the story came alive. The hollow echo of footsteps. The distant train horn. The crackling speaker announcements. The soft buzz of fluorescent bulbs. The quiet wind sliding across the empty platform. The rhythmic clatter of the approaching train. Together, these sounds created a world—one that felt real, lived-in, emotional.

He added a soft soundtrack beneath the ambient noise, carefully balancing the two so the music never drowned out the authenticity of the scene. Every footstep hit in sync with the character's movement. Every flicker of the lights had a subtle audio accent. When the train arrived, he added a low-frequency rumble to give weight to the moment. When Noah finished editing, he played the scene repeatedly, mesmerized. It felt like a short film. It felt like cinema. And it had nothing to do with fancy effects or expensive equipment. It was the sound.

The video went viral—not for visuals, but for emotion. Comments poured in praising the "soundscape," the "atmosphere," the "feeling of being there." Noah was stunned. He had spent years focusing solely on visuals, never realizing the secret ingredient for immersion was sound. The praise wasn't just validating—it was transformative. Sound was no longer background. It was storytelling.

From then on, Noah approached every video with new intention. He captured ambience at every location. He listened for emotional tones. He timed transitions to sound. He layered subtle effects to enhance realism. He treated sound design like painting—with frequencies instead of colors. And each video he created after that night felt richer, deeper, more alive.

The city had always spoken. Noah just hadn't listened. But once he did, he never forgot the lesson: visuals show the world, but sound makes you feel it.

Chapter 10

Cinematic Sequences: How to Build Story-Driven B-Roll That Feels Professional, Cohesive, and Emotionally Engaging

Cinematic sequences are the culmination of everything you've learned—composition, lighting, movement, pacing, color, sound, transitions, and visual effects—all working together toward one unified purpose: storytelling. While individual shots may look beautiful on their own, true cinematic quality emerges only when shots connect gracefully, emotionally, and intentionally. A cinematic sequence is not just a series of clips; it is a visual narrative. It is a moment that unfolds with structure and rhythm. It has a beginning, a middle, and an end—even if it is only five to ten seconds long. In modern content creation, especially on YouTube, Instagram, and TikTok, cinematic sequences grab attention, elevate branding, increase retention, and deepen emotional impact. They turn ordinary footage into an experience.

The foundation of a cinematic sequence is structure. Every sequence should follow a natural progression. Typically, this progression involves establishing context, focusing on detail, building atmosphere, and delivering a satisfying visual resolution. For example, a coffee-making sequence might open with a wide shot of the kitchen, transition into mid-shots of hands preparing ingredients, then move into tight macro shots of steam, textures, and pours, and end with a finished cup presented in a beautiful frame. This structure provides the viewer a sense of movement and evolution. Without structure, footage feels random. With structure, it feels purposeful, cinematic, and emotionally resonant.

Another essential element of cinematic sequences is shot variety. You cannot build a compelling sequence out of three shots that all look the same. You need angles—wide shots for context, medium shots for action, tight shots for emotional texture, macro shots for intimacy, and transitional shots that move the story forward. Shot variety is visual vocabulary. Each angle communicates a different feeling. Wide shots create breath and space. Tight shots create intensity and focus. Movement creates immersion. The more variety you capture, the more editorial possibilities you gain. And the more possibilities you have, the more fluidly you can shape a cinematic sequence.

Pacing is the heartbeat of your sequence. Good pacing feels invisible; bad pacing feels mechanical. Rapid pacing can energize the viewer, while slower pacing creates mood, reflection, or introspection. The key is matching pacing to emotional tone. A fitness sequence may feature quick cuts, speed ramps, and rhythmic movements. A travel moment might lean into slow motion, long dissolves, and ambient sound. A product advertisement may mix both styles depending on brand personality. Pacing is not about speed—it's about emotional alignment. Each sequence should have rising action, peak action, and a visual settling point. This rise-and-fall pattern is what creates engagement.

Color and lighting unify sequences visually. Even slight mismatches in exposure or color temperature can make sequences feel disjointed. Consistent lighting direction, color grading, and contrast give your sequence harmony. You might choose warm tones for cozy lifestyle content, cool tones for modern tech content, high contrast for dramatic action, or pastel palettes for soft aesthetics. The key is choosing a color mood and sticking to it throughout the sequence. When every clip feels like part of the same world, your sequence becomes cinematic.

Transitions are the connective tissue. They can be subtle or pronounced, but they must feel intentional. Cutting on action, matching movement, using soft wipes, incorporating foreground objects, or using natural scene changes ensures continuity. Even simple hard cuts become cinematic when done with rhythm and precision. Transitions should guide the viewer emotionally rather than distract. They should feel like natural breaths between shots, not forced disruptions. Well-planned transitions elevate your sequence into professional storytelling.

Sound design adds depth, dimension, and realism. Layering ambience, foley, music, and subtle motion accents transforms silent visuals into immersive experiences. A cinematic sequence without sound is hollow. Sound completes the illusion of reality. When your audio aligns with pacing, transitions, and emotional tone, your sequence becomes much more powerful. Slow sequences benefit from subtle ambience and gentle music. Fast sequences thrive on rhythmic beats and energetic accents. Sound is the invisible layer that binds everything together.

Finally, the key to building cinematic sequences is intentionality. Every shot must have a purpose. Every transition must feel natural. Every sound must support emotion. Every color must reinforce tone. Every detail must guide the viewer's eye. Cinematic storytelling is not about complexity—it is about clarity. It is about crafting a moment that feels alive, meaningful, and unified. When your sequences follow emotional logic and artistic intention, your content rises above the noise and becomes unforgettable.

Creating cinematic sequences is not a technical challenge; it is a mindset. It is the practice of seeing beauty in progression, rhythm in movement, and story in moments most people overlook. Once you learn this language, every room, every object, every action becomes an opportunity for visual storytelling. And your videos begin to reflect the filmmaker you truly are.

The Sequence He Didn't Know He Was Making

Theo wasn't trying to make a cinematic sequence. He was just trying to make tea. It was a cold Saturday morning, and he had decided to film a simple lifestyle reel for fun—a warm drink, soft window light, quiet music. Nothing complicated. Nothing dramatic. But as he placed the kettle on the stove, something caught his eye—the way the steam curled into the pale light, the way the gold rim of the mug glowed softly, the way the shadows danced on the counter. Without thinking, he picked up his phone and filmed a few seconds. Then he filmed the water filling the kettle. Then the flame igniting under the pot. Then the tea bag dipping into the mug. One moment flowed into another.

He didn't realize he was building a cinematic sequence. But something inside him did.

When he looked back at the raw footage, he paused. Individually, the clips were simple. But together, they felt like a story—a quiet morning ritual, calm and intimate. Theo leaned forward, replaying the clips in order. He saw structure where he hadn't intended any: a beginning (lighting the stove), a middle (the transformation of water into tea), and an end (the steaming mug resting in warm light). He felt something unexpected—a sense that he had captured a moment rather than a task.

He edited the clips with curiosity. He added a soft piano track. He slowed the steam to half speed. He brightened the highlights to make the tea glow. He added a gentle whoosh to transition from one shot to the next. Then he placed a wide shot at the beginning—a simple view of the quiet kitchen. The sequence now had breath, rhythm, emotion. It felt like a memory. It felt like something a filmmaker would create.

Theo posted the video expecting nothing. But the reaction stunned him. Thousands of people commented on how peaceful it felt. How warm. How "cinematic." They wrote about how the sequence transported them back to their own quiet mornings. How they could "almost smell the tea." Theo sat still, reading the reactions. He had never set out to create something meaningful. He had only followed curiosity. But curiosity, he realized, was the beginning of every great sequence.

Encouraged, he began filming other daily rituals. Folding clothes. Opening curtains. Writing in a notebook. Watering plants. Cooking dinner. But this time, he filmed with intention. He framed wide establishing shots. He captured close-ups of textures. He used movement to transition between steps. He matched color tones throughout the scene. He layered ambient sound—the rustle of fabric, the flick of switches, the clink of mugs. Each sequence felt more cohesive, more emotional, more cinematic.

Then came the day that changed everything. Theo visited his grandmother's home to help her cook a family recipe—one she had made for decades. He filmed from the moment she tied her apron to the moment the dish was placed on the table. Flour dust drifting through sunlight. Her hands kneading dough. The slow pour of sauce. The quiet concentration in her eyes. Steam rising from the finished dish. When he edited the sequence, he realized he hadn't just filmed cooking—he had filmed legacy.

The final video made him emotional. It wasn't flashy. It wasn't complex. But it was real. It had structure, rhythm, and heart. It felt like a love letter to his grandmother. He added a soft piano melody, gentle ambient sound, and a warm color grade. The sequence held memories in every frame.

He posted it, unsure how others would react. The response overwhelmed him. People wrote about their own grandparents, their own recipes, their own memories. They shared stories. They thanked him. They told him the video touched them. It was then Theo understood the true power of cinematic sequences. They weren't about gear or special effects. They were about capturing emotion. Capturing connection. Capturing humanity. He had never planned to be a filmmaker, but in that moment, he realized he already was.

And every time he filmed a new sequence—whether simple or profound—he remembered that the most cinematic moments are the ones life already gives you. Your job is only to see them ... and let them unfold.

Epilogue

The Cinematic Creator You Know You Can Become

Every creator begins with a camera and a desire to share something—an idea, a moment, a skill, a feeling. But cinematic storytelling demands more than simply hitting "record." It demands intention. It asks you to see the world differently, to observe light, motion, color, sound, texture, and atmosphere with the curiosity of an artist and the precision of a filmmaker. Throughout this book, you have explored the tools and techniques that elevate your content—not because they are trendy, but because they are timeless elements of visual communication. From purposeful B-roll to seamless transitions, from emotional color grading to immersive sound design, from thoughtful composition to subtle visual effects, you've learned that great filmmaking is not built on complexity. It is built on awareness.

Cinematic content does not emerge from equipment—it emerges from the way you perceive your environment. Once you understand light, you stop waiting for it to be "good" and instead learn to shape it. Once you understand movement, you stop filming randomly and begin filming with flow, rhythm, and intention. Once you understand color, you stop hoping for mood and begin sculpting it. Every tool becomes an extension of your eye. Every choice becomes deliberate. And this intention becomes your signature—a visual identity your audience will subconsciously recognize and trust.

You now understand that cinematic storytelling is not reserved for filmmakers with massive studios. It belongs equally to the creator filming in a small bedroom, the traveler shooting from a phone, the business owner recording product B-roll with simple lighting, or the artist capturing emotion in everyday moments. In the world of digital content, your camera is the least important element. Your vision is everything. Even the smallest details—light falling across a cup, shadows moving slowly on a wall, footsteps echoing through a hallway—can become cinematic when framed with intention. The magic was never hidden. It simply required you to see it.

As you continue creating, you will discover that cinematic mastery is not a destination but a continuous refinement. You will replay your early videos and smile at how far you've come. You will experiment with techniques you once felt intimidated by and find them second nature. You will build sequences that feel uniquely yours—moments shaped by emotion, color, pacing, and rhythm. Your audience will connect with your work more deeply, not because it looks expensive, but because it feels alive. The greatest gift of cinematic filmmaking is that it teaches you to appreciate ordinary beauty. The way sunlight hits a countertop. The comforting glow of a lamp. The texture of fabric moving in the wind. The reflection in a puddle after rain. The soft crackle of a candle. The quiet hum of a city at night. Once you train your eyes to notice these moments, you begin to see stories everywhere—not in grand scenes but in the subtle poetry of daily life. Cinematic creators don't wait for extraordinary subjects. They transform ordinary ones into extraordinary experiences.

This journey has prepared you to create content that resonates, captivates, and endures. You now have the vocabulary—visual, emotional, technical—to craft videos that rise above trends and leave lasting impressions. Whether you're filming short-form content, long-form tutorials, travel reels, product demos, lifestyle moments, or branded campaigns, the principles inside this book will guide you. They will anchor your style. They will refine your instincts. And they will remind you that cinematic artistry is always within reach.

Your next video is an opportunity. An experiment. A canvas. A moment. Use the tools you've learned. Trust your eye. Follow your intuition. Allow your creativity to speak. And remember that the world is full of beauty waiting for a lens—your lens—to reveal it. This is not the end of your cinematic journey. It is the beginning of a new creative identity. One shaped by intention, elevated by artistry, and driven by the simple truth that the most powerful stories often come from the most unexpected places. Keep filming. Keep exploring. And keep creating magic—one frame at a time.